Confiden In Christian Ministry

by
Andrew P. Marsden

Assistant Curate, St. John's, Newport, Isle of Wight

gb GROVE BOOKS LIMITED
Bramcote   Nottingham   NG9 3DS

CONTENTS

	Page
Introduction	3
1. Secrecy	5
2. The Moral Justification for Confidentiality	11
3. Limits to the Application of Confidentiality	15
4. The Seal of Confession	20
Bibliography	25

THE COVER PICTURE

is by William Smith

First Impression October 1993

ISSN 0951–2667

ISBN 1 85174 248 4

INTRODUCTION

All of us have secrets. We each have parts of ourselves which we hide from others. Some things about ourselves we never reveal. Others we tell only to trusted friends or relatives. All of us has secrets to keep. They may be our own secrets, or secrets entrusted to us by others. Confidentiality is integral to all human relationships, and thus to the functioning of society as a whole.

We are all asked to keep confidences. But there are those whose role in society means that they are privy to much more confidential information than others: doctors, lawyers, teachers, psychiatrists and many others. Indeed the principle of 'professional' confidentiality is an old one. The ancient works of Hindu medicine mention the obligation to medical secrecy, while in the Hippocratic Oath the newly-fledged Greek physician promised the following:

> 'What I may see or hear in the course of treatment or even outside the treatment in regard to the life of men, which on no account one must spread abroad, I will keep to myself, holding such things shameful to be spoken about.' (cit. Walters, p.198)

There can be little doubt that clergy, too, have an obligation to professional confidentiality. Most prominent in the public mind is probably the absolute confidentiality attached to the seal of confession. But it is not only in the context of formal confession that the need for confidentiality arises for the Christian minister. The office of the clergy person encourages confidences even in general pastoral ministry. Moreover, many clergy are involved in pastoral counselling or spiritual direction, where it is necessary for individuals to be open about themselves if they are to be helped towards healing and spiritual growth.

It is not only the clergy who are engaged in pastoral ministry in our churches, and who are likely to be told things in confidence. The same is true of readers, pastoral assistants, house group leaders, youth leaders, counsellors and any others who have a recognized role within church life which has a pastoral dimension. How does a youth leader react when a fourteen-year-old reveals privately that she is on drugs but does not want her parents to know? What about the teacher who tells his house group leader that he has sexual fantasies about the children under his care? Are these pieces of information to be kept absolutely confidential, or are there limits to confidentiality?

As far as I am aware nothing has yet been written to help the Christian minister in such a situation. There are some guidelines about the exercise of confidentiality in pastoral ministry, but these usually deal with practical issues rather than the ethics of confidentiality itself. This booklet therefore attempts to answer some basic questions. What is secrecy? How is it related to morality? What is the ethical basis for confidentiality? Under what circumstances might there be limits to confidentiality? The final chapter deals with the 'seal of the confessional', which is often asserted, but rarely justified from an ethical point of view. At every stage I have tried to place the issues in a Biblical and theological context.

3

I am aware that there are other areas which I might have considered. In the last two years the treatment of the royal family by the press has raised urgent questions about media confidentiality. The whole area of data protection is also one which is very relevant to any consideration of the ethics of confidentiality. Some of the material in this booklet is relevant to these issues, but most of it is focused on the issues of confidentiality encountered in Christian ministry. It does not attempt to provide easy answers to difficult situations, but rather to give an ethical and theological framework within which to set individual cases which are encountered in pastoral ministry.

1. SECRECY

Secrecy and Morality

Our word 'secret' comes from the Latin *secernere*, which means to sift, separate or set apart. The verb thus implies discernment, the making of distinctions, and the difference between insiders and outsiders. The noun, *secretum*, may suggest sacredness, intimacy, or privacy, but also prohibition, furtiveness, and deception. The Latin *arcanum* literally means something which is 'shut up' (as in a chest, *arca*), but came to refer more specifically to religious or divine secrets. In the German *heimlich* and Dutch *heimelijk* secrecy is connected with the home (*Heim*), the private sphere. The Greek *arrētos* has the connotation of that which cannot or should not be said because it is shameful, dishonourable or abominable.

It is clear that the concept of secrecy carries a range of moral nuances. At one end of the scale, secrecy is sometimes connected with divine mysteries, while at the other it carries connotations of shame and dishonour. Sissela Bok points out that, whatever one's moral principles, secrecy has a near paradoxical relationship with them: 'It may prevent harm, but it follows maleficence like a shadow.' (Bok, p.28).

Thus, on the one hand, secrecy may be a form of protection. In counselling or psychotherapy the client is encouraged to reveal intimate details about his or her life. Confidentiality is essential in order to ensure the client that this information will not be misused. We might also argue that secrecy is sometimes necessary in public institutions. The police would find it difficult to carry out their duties without being able to preserve a certain element of secrecy about their operations. The same is true of an organization like MI5. In recent calls for the security services to be more accountable to parliament there has been no question of details of their actual operations being revealed to the select committee. It is generally accepted by Members of Parliament that this is an area where secrecy must be preserved for the proper functioning of a service which is in the public interest.

On the other hand, however, secrecy is a cloak which may conceal evil along with good. It may be used to harm others rather than to benefit them. Where secrecy gives freedom of choice to one individual, it may limit or destroy that of others. It was in Robert Maxwell's interest to keep secret the huge sums he had diverted from his employees' pension funds, but hardly in the interests of the pensioners who have suffered as a consequence. In that secrecy guards against inspection and interference, it is central to the planning of any act which will injure other human beings. There is secrecy involved in planning a bank robbery or a computer fraud, but only the criminals themselves would argue that such secrecy is justified.

On another level, secrecy can debilitate judgement, by shutting out criticism and allowing people to maintain facades which conceal their true character. There have been cases in the past of convicted child molesters being given jobs involving the care of children simply because they kept quiet about their criminal record. Even though a check in police records is now mandatory, an applicant with a history of child abuse but no previous conviction might still be offered a job in childcare. In such a case the cloak of secrecy hides the true character of the applicant and deprives the employer of information which would affect his or her judgement.

A Biblical Perspective

In the Bible we find a similar paradox in the way secrecy is regarded. The main thrust of both the Old and New Testaments is that ours is a God who reveals himself. He is known first of all as the God of Abraham, Isaac, and Jacob, and later reveals himself to Moses under his name, Yaweh. He reveals his will through the detailed laws of the Pentateuch and through his prophetic messengers. Amos could write: 'Surely the Sovereign LORD does nothing without revealing his plan to his servants the prophets' (Amos 3.7). His character, too, was apparent from his commands and from his actions. Here is a continuing process of revelation, culminating in the incarnation. The Christian God is by his nature the One who reveals himself, and that supremely in his Son, the Logos.

Yet the very fact that God's revelation is progressive shows that at any one time there are things which he conceals from human beings. In the account of the renewal of the covenant in Deuteronomy Moses ends with the words: 'The secret things belong to the LORD our God, but the things revealed belong to us and to our children for ever, that we may follow all the words of this law' (29.29). Certain matters of eternal significance belong to God alone, while others are revealed to human beings. Enough is revealed to the Israelites to enable them to keep their side of the covenant.

Not that God is deliberately concealing parts of his character in order to deceive us. When God restricts his revelation it is for our own good. When Moses asked to see the glory of God, it was only the 'back' of God that was revealed to him, since 'no one may see me and live' (Exodus 33.20). Jesus commented to his disciples that there were many things he could teach them, but which at that time they would not be able to grasp (John 16.12). On this earth our knowledge of God is restricted, but it will not always be so. As Paul put it: 'Now we see but a poor reflection as in a mirror; then we shall see face to face. Now I know in part; then I shall know fully, even as I am fully known.' (1 Corinthians 13.12).

When God reveals or chooses not to reveal he does so out of love for human beings. Thomas Aquinas reminds us that 'The Son...is the Word, but not simply any kind of word, but the word breathing forth love' (cit. Haring, p.10). This is an important truth which must lie behind any consideration of the ethics of communication. If the imitation of Christ is the goal of the Christian life, then the way that we appropriate and use knowledge must be grounded in love. Our silence, as much as our words, must express that love for God and neighbour which Christ commanded and which he demonstrated.

The divine Word made flesh in Jesus Christ was not only an expression of love, but also of truth. Christ came to bear witness to the truth (John

18.36-38), and is himself that truth (John 14.6). The Holy Spirit is the Spirit of truth, who bears witness to the truth of Christ (John 14.15-17,26). To be possessed by the divine truth and to bear witness to it is a prerequisite for worship (Psalm 15). Our very lives are to be an expression of the good, perfect and pleasing will of God (Romans 12.1-2). Just as God's truth limits us in what we do, so it may also limit us in what we say. Thus silence may be an expression of divine truth. In the words of Bonhoeffer, 'the assigned purpose of our silence is to signify the limit which is imposed upon our words by the real as it exists in God' (Bonhoeffer, p.332).

Yet in a fallen world we do not always find it easy to communicate in this way. As James put it, our tongue is a restless fire with great potential for evil. Out of the same mouth come praise and cursing. Out of the same spring come both fresh and salt water. Bonhoeffer comments:
> 'In our efforts to express the real we do not encounter this as a consistent whole, but in a condition of disruption and inner contradiction which has need of reconciliation and healing. We find ourselves simultaneously embedded in various different orders of the real, and our words, which strive towards the reconciliation and healing of the real, are nevertheless repeatedly drawn into the prevalent disunion and conflict. They can indeed fulfil their assigned purpose of expressing the real, as it is in God, only by taking up into themselves both the inner contradiction and the inner consistency of the world. If the words of men are to be true they must deny neither the Fall nor God's word of creation and reconciliation, the word in which all disunion is overcome.' (Bonhoeffer, p.332).

As we seek to 'express the real as it exists in God' we come up against 'the truth that since the Fall there has been a need also for concealment and secrecy' (Bonhoeffer, p.334). This is the secrecy which 'shadows maleficence'. It is only after the Fall that Adam and Eve are lead to *conceal* their nakedness and to *hide* from God (Gen. 3.8). This secrecy arises from fear (Gen. 3.10) and shame (cf. Gen 2.25). It is a constant theme throughout the Bible that our sins separate us from God (eg. Is. 59.2) and the light of Christ exposes sins which are done in secret (Eph. 5.8-14). Here that which is done in secret is seen as shameful, and it will be made visible by God (cf. Rom. 2.16; 1 Cor. 14.25).

Yet in a fallen world secrecy does not always conceal that which is evil. It can be the tool of reconciliation and healing as well as a cloak for evil deeds. It was for this reason that Jesus counselled secrecy in almsgiving, prayer, and fasting (Mt. 6.1-8, 16-18). Here secrecy ensures the purity of our motives. When we do our good deeds in secret we cannot be seeking the approval of other human beings, since God alone 'sees what is done in secret' (Mt. 6.4). Secrecy is a powerful instrument which we may wield either to express God's creating and reconciling love, or to further that division and destruction of human beings and their self-respect which is the antithesis of God's Word of love expressed in Jesus Christ.

The Secret in Moral Theology
On the grounds that secrecy will sometimes be necessary for the Christian in a fallen world, Roman Catholic moral theology has defined secrecy as

'something hidden, which it is one's duty to keep concealed' (Regan, p.1). This assumes a second person knowing one's secret, and Regan points out that the most basic secret is that which is locked in the human heart. He therefore revises the definition:

'A secret is some hidden knowledge, pertaining to a person by strict right, which another may not lawfully seek to possess, use, or dispose of (i.e. reveal) contrary to the reasonable will of the owner' (Regan, p.3)

Thus moral theologians regard a secret as a possession: something which belongs to one person but may be stolen and used by another. They have generally distinguished three types of secret:

1. The natural secret. Into this category fall any secrets which, if revealed, would harm the owner of the secret. Thus if one were to learn another person's PIN number this would come into the category of a natural secret. Another example might be the knowledge that a person is HIV positive. Thus it is the very nature of the hidden knowledge which makes it a natural secret. Regardless of how one has come into possession of such knowledge, its character dictates that it should not be revealed under normal circumstances. The obligation to keep such secrets rests on the command to love our neighbour and not to do to others what we would not want them to do to us. It needs no contract to make it binding.

2. The promised secret. This covers hidden truths or facts which one is told but which one subsequently promises not to reveal. The promise must be made freely and not under coercion. The secret itself need not be of the nature of a natural secret. If a child tells you where he or she has hidden an Easter egg in the garden, and you promise not to reveal the location, then this comes into the category of a promised secret. It is the promise itself which makes this secret binding rather than the nature of what one is told.

3. The entrusted (or committed) secret. In this case the promise not to reveal the secret is made prior to disclosure. The entrusted secret has a contractual nature and it may be explicit or implicit. It is explicit if a promise of secrecy is formally requested before the secret is disclosed. It is implicit when the office or function of the person to whom the secret is being revealed makes it clear that the secret will be carefully guarded. Into this category, for example, would fall information revealed to lawyers, doctors, psychiatrists, and of course clergy. The implicit entrusted secret is therefore known as the *official secret* or, more recently, the *professional secret.*

The Professional Secret
This is the category of secret which applies most directly to the Christian minister. It will cover any hidden truths or facts revealed to a minister by virtue of his office. The hidden truths or facts may be very personal to the individual, and here professional secrecy may well be protecting natural secrets, in other words a person's privacy. However, such secrecy may also be protecting matters which are in no way private, but which the person wishes to keep from third parties. In general terms, confidentiality refers to the boundaries surrounding shared secrets and the process of guarding those boundaries.

Conditions under which a professional secret is binding:

1. The recipient of the secret must exercise a public or quasi-public function or office in society. The function or office concerned must be of a fiduciary nature, in other words it must be one that invites or involves confidential communications. Finally, the function or office must be one that is necessary, or at least very useful, to the common welfare.

   In Christian ministry this definition would cover not only the priest or pastor, but also all those who are commissioned to undertake pastoral ministry. In the Church of England it would apply to Lay Readers and other licensed lay workers. It would also apply to those who are not officially licensed, but who have clear pastoral functions within the local church. Examples would be House Group Leaders, Youth leaders, and those involved in counselling or healing ministries.

2. As far as the confidence itself is concerned, it must not already be common or public knowledge, and it must be matter for a valid secret. An invalid secret would be one which is directed towards an evil purpose, such as the revelation of the intent to commit a crime. A minister or other professional cannot validly contract to keep secret such a confidence. Under these circumstances the implicit promise or contract would be invalid, and the minister not bound by it. Clearly there are problems of definition here. Space precludes a detailed discussion of what constitutes 'evil purpose', but at the very least it encompasses an intention to do something which will cause serious physical or emotional harm to an innocent third party or parties.

The scope of the professional secret:

In scope the professional secret covers all matters of a secret nature which the professional learns about from his or her client during the exercise of his profession. In theory moral theology distinguishes between secrets learnt about *by reason of* his or her profession, and those learnt on the occasion of the exercise of his or her profession. The former would come into the category of a professional secret, whilst the latter would not (though it might be material for a natural secret).

In practice this is a difficult distinction to draw. It is clear that in the counselling room or on a pastoral visit information is being revealed to the minister by reason of his office. But does the same apply to facts revealed over a cup of coffee after church? Perhaps the nature of the occasion is the best guide. The cup of coffee after church is primarily a social occasion, as is the church barbecue or Christmas party. It seems fair to argue that information revealed to a minister on such an occasion does not come into the category of professional secret. However, the nature of the information might well make it a natural secret, and the minister feel bound to confidentiality in any case.

The obligation to professional secrecy is normally regarded as perpetual, even after the death of the client. It covers not only the words spoken by the client, but also his or her expressions and physical demeanour. It covers favourable as well as unfavourable information about the client.

The fact itself of a person seeking professional aid is not normally seen as a professional secret. However there may be grounds for regarding it as a natural secret, or for a promised secret. Since this may not be apparent at once, it seems advisable in any case to keep appointments and counselling sessions completely confidential.

Persons bound by the professional secret:
Normally professional secrecy is thought of as a right and a duty existing between two individuals. In more modern times few professional people do their work unassisted, and so the obligation is extended to lawyer's clerks, laboratory technicians and so on. The minister, however, still largely works alone, and some would insist that the client's permission should be sought if he or she wants to consult another minister or professional.

However, some theologians have argued that it is valid to reveal an entrusted secret to another prudent person, provided that person is really prudent, that he or she is placed under the same obligation of entrusted secrecy, and is not the very person from whom the secret was supposed to be withheld. Cocina objects to this that the person concerned could pass on the secret to someone else on the same terms, and so on until a whole group of people knew the secret. Regan suggests the extra condition that the person revealing the secret must be morally certain that it will go no further.

On this basis it is possible to argue that a minister might reveal the secret to his or her spouse, or to a close friend unconnected with the situation, provided he or she is morally certain that the information will go no further. The same would apply to a curate wishing to seek advice on a particular case from his vicar, or a parish priest or deacon who wanted to consult the Rural Dean or Archdeacon. This is a particularly important in a counselling situation where another person's perspective may be of considerable help in forwarding the counselling. It may also help the counsellor to share the emotional burden with another.

It is common practice in secular counselling organizations to extend the boundaries of confidentiality beyond the individual counsellor. In Relate, for example, cases are discussed in detail with one's supervisor, and may also be discussed with other counsellors within the organization, provided no names are revealed. However, clients should be aware of this fact in advance, and in the same way it is advisable for the Christian minister involved in counselling to tell parishioners beforehand if cases are likely to be discussed with another person.

2. THE MORAL JUSTIFICATION FOR CONFIDENTIALITY

So far the obligation to professional secrecy has been defined in terms which assume that it is morally justified. Although we touched on the question of secrecy and moral choice above, it is now necessary to deal in some detail with the arguments usually put forward to justify confidentiality in ethical terms. Two specific arguments of a deontological nature are usually said to support a *prima facie* case for confidentiality: the need to respect the autonomy of the individual; and the need to preserve the character of human relationships. These are supported by any promise of secrecy which is made. Finally professional secrecy as such is justified on the basis of the contract with the client, and on the consequentialist argument that the efficient functioning of the professional-client relation would be impeded without it.

Protection of Individual Autonomy

At the most basic level confidentiality protects our sense of self. Van Asperen stresses the importance of an awareness of the differences between ourselves and others. To develop a sense of self is to develop a sphere of one's own to which others may be admitted but which they need permission to enter. What we mean by respect for a person has to do, partly, with respect for this hidden inner core. For Van Asperen part of the process of growing up is the development of such a sense of self, whilst an inability to distinguish between self and the outside world is often a sign of mental instability or psychosis. She asserts that in a normal grown up life openness and secrecy need to be balanced, even though this balance may be different in different cultures and societies. We might also affirm that this balance between openness and secrecy will vary from individual to individual even in the same culture or society. Nevertheless her basic point is valid. Human beings are created with a sense of self, a sense of identity. We are created in the image of God, and like him we need to be able to say 'I am'. One of the functions of confidentiality is to protect this basic right.

Integral to this sense of identity is the fact that we are created so that our thoughts are inviolable to other human beings. However, when our thoughts are laid bare it is not only our sense of identity which is violated. Depending on the nature and extent of the revelation, degrees of self-government or personal freedom may also be affected. Our freedom of action may be curtailed. Many projects, like diplomacy or other sensitive negotiations, require confidential planning if they are to be carried out effectively. Alternatively, our right to hold personal property may be violated. If the knowledge of our possessions or their whereabouts is revealed then they are more vulnerable to being stolen.

In fact secrecy protects whatever individual right might be violated by our thoughts being laid bare. When our intentions and plans are revealed we are more easily controlled by others. In totalitarian regimes spies and informants thrive, since it is control of information about individuals which is central to suppressing any deviation from the party line. In George Orwell's *1984* it was the all-seeing eye of Big Brother which so much curtailed human freedom. It is for this reason that Sissela Bok argues that conflicts over secrecy are essentially conflicts over power.

11

In essence, therefore, secrecy protects the individual's right to self-government, to personal freedom, or autonomy. For Bok confidentiality is a means of enabling individuals to retain control over personal information: 'Control over secrecy provides a safety valve for individuals in the midst of communal life—some influence over transactions between the world of personal experience and the world shared with others' (Bok, p.20). Moral theologians think along similar lines, but speak of 'ownership' rather than 'control' of a secret. A secret is considered to be the property of its owner, who can therefore possess, use and dispose of his secret in any lawful manner. Violation of the secret contravenes the command not to steal. Van Asperen writes in similar terms that just as an invitation to a house does not give one the right to start selling the furniture, so an invitation to glimpse someone's inner life does not give one the right to make it public.

However, just as property rights have their limitations, so the right to secrets is limited by just law, the rights of others, and the exigencies of the social order. This covers the situations where it is more difficult to decide who owns the information, as with the driver of the school bus who has a heart condition. In Roman Catholic moral theology, however, these limitations apply more to natural secrets than to promised or professional secrets. The professional secret is said to give the owner a strict right that his secret will not be not unduly appropriated.

Protection of the Character of Human Relationships

If confidentiality protects our sense of self, then it also protects our right to share that inner self with others. It protects, in fact, our ability to live in relationship with each other. In Genesis God said 'It is not good for the man to be alone.' (2.18). We are relational beings, and as such we reflect not only the image of God who is one, but also the image of God the Holy Trinity. The relationship between Father, Son and Holy Spirit is free and open, but in a fallen world our relationships need protection. We cannot trust all our acquaintances to respect our deeper secrets, and few of us have the emotional reserves to be on terms of intimacy with all of our friends.

Charles Fried suggests that privacy may be regarded as 'moral capital' which we spend in relationships of love, friendship and trust. Privacy, and by extension secrecy, provides us with the control over information which enables us to maintain degrees of intimacy. Sometimes the image of concentric circles or spheres is used. In the centre are the individual's 'ultimate secrets', which are beyond sharing except in a situation of extreme stress where they must be poured out to gain ultimate release. The next largest circle contains intimate secrets to be shared with close relatives or confessors of various kinds. Successively larger circles are open to intimate friends, to casual acquaintances, and finally to all observers.

Secrets therefore have a role to play in the way that human relationships function. Human society cannot function properly without an obligation to respect the secrets of others. Some writers see this respect for the secrets of others as being built upon loyalty to the collective survival of tribe, clan or kin. For Van Asperen to be a member of a group means 'being reliable', 'proving oneself trustworthy'. As Christians we might rather say that being a member of the human race should mean 'being reliable', 'proving oneself trustworthy'. It is not the way society functions, but the way God intends it to function, which should be the basis of our morality. The parable of the Good Samaritan makes it clear that love for neighbour is to include not only our close associates but all of humanity.

To suggest that respect for the secrets of others is rooted in a loyalty to group or tribe is to base one's morality on the divisions between class and race which the Bible makes clear are a result of the Fall. Christ came to destroy the 'dividing wall of hostility' (Eph. 2.14) not only between Jew and Gentile, but between all groups of human beings which set themselves up one against the other. Criminal organizations like the Mafia are based on collective loyalty and shared secrets, but no one would suggest that the activities which they protect are morally justifiable. We do have a responsibility to respect the secrets of others, but this responsibility is based not on collective loyalty to a particular group, but on obedience to God's moral law.

The Promise of Secrecy
A pledge of silence creates an obligation beyond the respect due to persons and to existing relationships. Once we promise someone secrecy we introduce an extra factor into our moral deliberations about a situation. In promising we alienate, as Grotius said, either a thing or a portion of our freedom of action: 'To the former category belong promises to give, to the latter promises to perform.' (cit. Bok, p.120). In the case of a promise of secrecy, what we promise to give is allegiance, and what we promise to perform is some action which will guard the secret (at the least to keep silent). For many people a promise involves their integrity, and a promise to secrecy is sometimes invested with a special meaning, in part at least because of the respect for persons and relationships which is called for in our first two premises. Nevertheless, questions still arise about whether it was right to make the promise in the first place, and right to accept it; whether the promise is binding, and even if it is, what circumstances might justify overriding it.

Roman Catholic moral theology makes a distinction between a promise made after hearing the secret, and that made before. In the case of the former, the merely promised secret, there is clearly a contractual obligation to secrecy but theologians are divided over the force of that obligation. Greater weight is assigned to the latter—the entrusted or professional secret—since there is a prior contract with the client, and since the secret itself is deemed to be useful to society as a whole.

Justification for Professional Secrecy
Professional confidentiality is also justified on the basis of the two moral arguments given above, namely that it protects the autonomy of the individual, and the character of human relationships. In this case,

however, two additional arguments are put forward which strengthen the obligation to confidentiality:

(1) The prior contract with the client. As mentioned above the professional person is seen as having a prior contract with the client that he will carefully guard secrets entrusted to him in the exercise of his office. In most cases the client may be said to have consented to the contract, though there are sometimes situations where there is a need to resort to the notion of an implicit contract, as with a surgeon who must operate on a person who is unconscious after an accident.

Such a contract lends extra weight to the justifications for confidentiality given above, because there is a prior commitment to keep secret whatever the client may reveal. The professional is aligning him or herself with the client as far as keeping the client's secrets is concerned.

(2) The good of society. Extra weight is also assigned to the obligation of the professional secret because it is necessary to the proper functioning of professions—like medicine, psychiatry, and the law—which benefit society as a whole. Individual human beings are not self-sufficient. They need recourse to others for help, and sometimes this might involve a good deal of self-revelation. Professional confidentiality enables clients to seek help they might otherwise fear to ask for, and the knowledge that what they reveal will be kept secret is therefore integral to the proper functioning of the professions concerned.

Any genuinely therapeutic relationship must be based on trust. The client must be able to entrust him or herself to a doctor or counsellor, for example, knowing that any secrets are safe with this person. As one psychiatrist put it:

> 'The patient in analysis must learn to free associate and to break down resistances to deal with unconscious threatening thoughts and feelings. To revoke secrecy after encouraging such risk-taking is to threaten all future interaction' (cit. Walters, p.199).

Whilst the minister is not involved in psychoanalysis as such, openness is equally important in pastoral counselling, and the rationale of confession is that all sins need to be confessed before God. If those who sought counselling or confession thought that their innermost feelings and sins were in danger of being revealed, then they would either not come in the first place, or would be less than frank in what they were prepared to share. A legitimate degree of professional secrecy is therefore justified by the argument that society as a whole would be harmed if those who seek professional help of this kind were not able to do so.

3. LIMITS TO THE APPLICATION OF CONFIDENTIALITY

It has already been suggested in passing that there may be situations in which strict confidentiality can no longer be applied. We have already considered the need to consult with colleagues in a team situation, and if this is likely then the client should know in advance, and all the team should be bound to keep confidence. There may be other situations, however, where revelation seems necessary. Such situations will be rare and all others avenues should have been pursued before a confidence is revealed without the client's consent. When it seems important that a secret be revealed the first step will be to ask the client to reveal it or to permit it to be revealed. If this fails then a decision must be made about whether or not it is morally justifiable to reveal the secret without his or her consent.

Revelation of a secret will only be justified if the original reason for keeping the secret is no longer valid. Confidentiality itself is justified on two grounds: the protection of individual autonomy and the protection of human relationships. If a confidence is to be shared then it must be because either or both of these two grounds for keeping the confidence no longer apply. In the case of professional confidentiality, however, this will not normally be enough to justify revelation. Here there is the prior contract with the client to consider, as well as the overall benefits of the confidential relationship to society. Before a professional secret can be revealed it should be clear that these two factors are also no longer valid.

Limits to Individual Autonomy
Confidentiality is said to preserve the individual's right to self-government, to personal freedom, or autonomy. But there may be times when that autonomy is in question. There are degrees of autonomy, and confidences by children, mentally incompetent persons, or those temporarily not fully capable of guiding their own affairs may create problems for the professional listener, especially if harm to the individual may be prevented by not respecting the secret. A well known example of such a dilemma for the doctor would be the under-age girl asking to be prescribed the pill. Even more difficult might be childhood pregnancies, or drug addiction among the young. Although the children concerned might be anxious to keep the situation from their parents, one might well ask whether children are sufficiently responsible to make their own decisions in such matters.

Roman Catholic moral theologians argue that in the case of natural and promised secrets one is obliged to rescue the owner of a secret from harm even if this involves revelation of the secret. This is based on the principle that an individual would be unreasonable if they objected to being protected in this way. Even in the case of the professional secret most moral theologians assume the owner's implicit consent in such a situation.

Although it is said that a person would be unreasonable if they objected to being saved from inflicting harm on themselves, it is not always easy to define what is 'reasonable' in this situation. Bok suggests that it might seem unreasonable to give away all of one's possessions to an exploitative guru or to abandon life-prolonging medical treatment, but she points out that the judgement is more difficult if the act has been carefully considered. It may be that the person giving away all their possessions wants to live the rest of their life as a contemplative, or the patient abandoning medical treatment has decided to cease delaying death because of an increasingly debilitating and painful disease. In such cases it is harder to prove that the patient's act is unreasonable, or that it is necessarily self-destructive from his or her point of view. There is always the danger of the professional, including the Christian minister, too readily assuming that the principles they hold dear, and to which they have dedicated their career, will be shared by others.

If the client's state of mind is difficult to define, so is the degree of harm to the client which will justify revelation of the secret. Even if the client's autonomy seems to be in question the degree of harm which the client is bringing upon him or herself may also seem to be relevant. Is a thirteen-year old girl involved in prostitution doing herself more harm then a fifteen-year old in a steady relationship? If the parents are to be told in either case, does it make a difference if the father is known to be violent? Such decisions are not easy; each case will present a different set of factors to be weighed and considered before a decision can be made.

Threats to the Character of Human Relationships
Although secrets are deemed to be an important factor in preserving the character of human relationships, this cannot apply when those very relationships are threatened. We cannot claim the same confidentiality for personal information when an innocent person from whom the secret is kept runs serious risks. When Jesus summarized the OT law about relationships he did it in terms of love: 'Love your neighbour as yourself'. Confidentiality cannot justifiably protect information which contravenes the command to love our neighbour. A natural or promised secret is not binding if the harm likely to be caused to an innocent third party by keeping the secret is greater than the harm which is likely to befall the owner if his or her secret is revealed.

This is certainly the case where serious physical or emotional harm to another person has either taken place or is likely to take place. A clear example would be that of child abuse. Here an innocent third party has been harmed, and there is the likelihood that other children may be harmed in the future as well. Under these circumstances the abuser does not retain the right to his secret. This is all the more the case since the person concerned is a child who cannot easily defend herself. The OT prophets make it very clear that we have a particular duty to protect the weak and vulnerable in society, those who cannot help themselves.

It is also arguable that the right to the secret is forfeit when an innocent third party will be indirectly harmed by that secret being kept confidential. An example often quoted by the medieval scholastics is that of a man with incurable and an highly contagious venereal disease who plans to marry without telling his fiancee about his condition. A modern parallel is perhaps to be found in those who are HIV-positive, but are unwilling to tell their partners or children. Another example might be those who envisage marriage but have a genetic predisposition which may in the future result in (incurable) illness, or have a history of mental instability.

16

It need not be individual human relationships which are seriously threatened. In some cases it may be society as a whole or in part which is threatened by the keeping of a particular secret. In this case the command to love one's neighbour takes on a corporate dimension. Thus one is justified in reporting a crime to the police not only in order to prevent or reduce the suffering of those against whom the crime has been committed, but also because it is in the interests of society that crimes are exposed and punished. Roman Catholic moral theologians have argued that it is both lawful and mandatory to reveal a secret (of any type) which would prevent a serious material or spiritual evil befalling the community. The argument here is based on the assumption that the good of the community always comes before the good of the individual, but only if the the goods concerned are comparable. Thus, a soldier might choose to die at his post to prevent a similar fate befalling his countrymen, but an individual should not seriously jeopardize his own spiritual life for the physical welfare of the community.

Limits to Professional Secrecy
(1) The contract with the client is invalid:
In the case of a professional secret there is a prior commitment on the part of the recipient of the secret not to reveal it. He or she has a particular duty to guard that secret because of the implied contract with the client. Whether or not the secret is a valid one, the professional has an independent commitment to keep that secret. However, he or she will be free to reveal the secret if the prior contract is invalid. This will be the case if it is a contract directed towards an evil purpose. The recipient of the secret cannot agree to keep secret something which is directed towards a future immoral end. Another consideration will be the degree of harm likely to be caused to an innocent third party if the secret is not revealed. The benefit obtained by revelation of the secret should be greater than the damage caused to the owner.

Thus if we consider the examples given above, it is clear that in many of them a professional would be justified in revealing the secret. The child abuser who speaks about his actions to a counsellor or Christian minister should not necessarily expect his secret to be kept. There is no valid contract here since there is a serious danger of harm to an innocent third party. In such circumstances the counsellor or minister would be an indirect accomplice in any future abuse, and no contract of confidentiality can be valid under such circumstances. The same would be true for the doctor in the case of the person who is HIV-positive or has a genetic disease but refuses to tell his or her partner or children.

In all these cases the prior contract is invalid and the professional is permitted to reveal the secret. He or she is not necessarily obliged to reveal the secret, although some professionals in this country are now obliged to do so in the case of child abuse. Following the Children Act 1989 some local authority employees, like teachers, are required to report cases of child abuse that come to their notice to the social services. Although this is a mandatory requirement, it is based upon the moral argument that where an innocent third party is likely to suffer serious harm the professional has a duty to do all in his or her power to prevent that harm.

A rather different situation in which the contract might be regarded as no longer valid would be if the professional person put his or her own life at risk through keeping the secret. Canon 113 of 1604 required parish priests in the Church of England to preserve the secrecy of the confessional, but excused them in the case of 'such crime as by the laws of this realm his own life may be called into question for concealing the same'. Although extremely unlikely in this country, there are some places in the world where this might still be true today, and in any case the danger to the life of the recipient of the secret might come from a source other than the state. The situation is quite unlikely, but were it to arise it seems clear that the recipient of the secret is not bound by a contract which might involve serious harm to him or herself. He or she may choose voluntarily to keep the secret, despite the risk, but is not bound to do so.

(2) Secrecy is likely to harm rather than benefit society:
The professional secret is also justified on the grounds that it is necessary to the proper functioning of certain professions which benefit society as a whole. Sometimes this argument is used to justify absolute confidentiality. The 1949 International Code of Medical Ethics made this sweeping claim: 'A doctor shall preserve absolute secrecy on all he knows about his patient because of the confidence entrusted in him.' (cit. Bok, p.123). Such statements are in danger of elevating professional confidentiality to a position where it is *hors concours,* and where the interests of clients or patients are considered paramount, to the exclusion of the moral rights of other people who may be affected.

In 1969 in the United States a young woman, Tatiana Tarasoff, was killed by a man who had earlier told his psychotherapist that he planned to do so. The psychotherapist had told the police, but not Miss Tarasoff or her family, and the police had not felt able to detain him. The courts held the therapist guilty of breaching a duty beyond that of confidentiality, and the case caused a lot of consternation among psychiatrists. The latter argued that it is hard to say whether a threat will be carried out or not, and that the majority are not. They also said that the duty to warn a potential victim threatens the trust between a therapist and his client: the therapeutic relationship must be inviolate if therapy is to stand a chance.

There are parallels with the British case of Beverly Allitt, a hospital nurse who was recently sentenced to life imprisonment for killing babies under her care. Here strict rules about the confidentiality of hospital records concealed the fact that Allitt was being treated for a psychiatric disorder in another part of the hospital. Had the rules about confidentiality not been applied in such a rigid manner a tragedy might have been averted. When interviewed by the media the hospital authorities used similar arguments to those of the psychotherapists in the Tarasoff case, stating that most people with that particular condition do not commit murder. The implication seems to be that though there was a small risk to the babies concerned, the confidentiality of medical records was more important.

In both cases the argument employed centres around the idea that confidentiality is a necessary condition for the fulfilment of the professional role. If we do not allow absolute confidentiality in the medical and psychiatric professions we harm not only the individuals who seek their assistance, but the institutions themselves, and, in that way, the quality of our society. It is equally arguable, however, that the abuse of professional confidentiality may do more harm in the long run to the professions concerned, as well as to society. If the public are to have confidence in the nursing profession, for example, they need to be confident that nurses are properly screened for psychiatric disorders which might be harmful to their patients. A legitimate degree of professional confidentiality is not the same as an *absolute* confidentiality where the rights of anyone other than the clients of the profession concerned are ignored.

Limits on the Way the Secret is Revealed
Where it is decided that a secret must be revealed, the way it is revealed is almost as important as the fact of revelation itself. Roman Catholic moral theologians have addressed this subject, and have suggested three guidelines to be followed in the case of lawful revelation. These guidelines assume that all reasonable efforts have been made to preserve the secret, including all reasonable efforts to persuade the client to remove the cause which might make revelation of the secret necessary.

Firstly, a professional secret should only be revealed to the extent necessary to meet the situation effectively. Thus if the bare revelation of a fact without a client's name would obviate the difficulty then this is all that should be revealed. Similarly, if an indirect revelation would suffice, then a direct revelation should not be made. The situation is analogous to that of a person defending himself against attack, in which he or she should only use the amount of force necessary to repulse the assailant.

Secondly, a professional secret should only be revealed to the person or persons with a strict right to the information. In the case of the engaged man with venereal disease, it is his fiancee only who should be told. If a minor is concerned it is the parents or guardians who should be told. In the Tarasoff case this guideline would require the therapist to have told Miss Tarasoff herself about the threat. We cannot know whether this would have prevented the murder, but at least Miss Tarasoff would have been forewarned, and therefore have a better chance of avoiding her assailant. In general we might say that it is permissible to reveal the secret to the person or persons who must know it in order for the threatening danger to be successfully averted. Thus, to ensure the safety of Miss Tarasoff it might have been necessary for both herself and the police to know about the man's threats.

Thirdly, those to whom a professional secret is revealed should equally regard the information revealed to them as an entrusted secret. Again the analogy is with only using as much force as is necessary to repel an attacker, and the intention is to preserve as much as possible the client's right to the secret. Thus if Beverly Allitt's nursing superiors had been told about her psychiatric disorder they would have been obliged to treat that information as a professional secret, as far as was consonant with the protection of the babies under her care. The aim would have been to preserve the confidentiality of Beverly's medical records as much as possible, whilst also averting any harm to the babies.

4. THE SEAL OF CONFESSION

History

In the early church public confession of sins seems to have been the norm, even in the case of quite secret sins. Confidentiality was respected, but not enforced in an absolute way. Thus Tertullian insisted that the knowledge of the sins a person had committed be confined to the congregation. Although the earliest reference to private confession seems to come in Origen, it became more common only in the fifth century. The first references to the seal in local legislation come at the Armenian Synod of Dovin (527) in the east and at the Council of Douzy (874) in the west. Although the nature of the seal was discussed by various writers and councils between the ninth and thirteenth centuries, it was not until the Fourth Lateran Council (1215) that there was a general ecclesiastical law forbidding the priest to betray the penitent 'either by word or sign or in any other way whatsoever.' (cit. *New Cath. Enc., IV*, p.134).

Even after 1215 the absolute nature of the seal was not universally accepted, and the scholastics continued to debate the issue throughout the medieval period. The majority followed Aquinas in advocating complete confidentiality, and it is this view which is reflected in the current canons of the Roman Catholic Church. Canon 889, section 1, reads: 'The sacramental seal is inviolable, and hence the confessor shall be most careful not to betray the penitent by any word or sign or in any other way.' (cit. Tiemann, p.20). Canon 2369 pronounces excommunication on the one who breaks the seal of the Confessional directly. The Confessor may only reveal what has been said in the Confessional if the penitent gives him permission to do so.

In the Church of England there is also a strong tradition of recognising the seal of confession. In Canon 113 of 1604, with regard to confession, the parish priest is not to reveal any 'crime or offence committed to his trust and secrecy (except they be such crime as by the laws of this realm his own life may be called into question for concealing the same) under pain of irregularity' (cit. Ross, p.69). Since English law does not protect the seal of the confessional, the new Canon B29 of 1969 did not include this stipulation, though a footnote reminds the reader that Canon 113 of 1604 has never been repealed. Canon 113, of course, had its exemptive clause, which has been interpreted as requiring the priest to disclose any type of treason, though the Latin version seems to suggest that the reason justifying disclosure is not danger to the priest, but public danger. However, it is notable that this clause was omitted in the wording of the Act of the Convocations of Canterbury and York of 29 April 1959, which was otherwise quite faithful to the wording of Canon 113.

Justification for the Seal of Confession

It is clear that where the church has upheld the absolute confidentiality of the confessional, this has not been done in an unthinking manner. The concept of the seal of confession as we find it today has developed over many years and is no arbitrary ruling. However, we stand today at some distance from the theological debate of the scholastics. In our own time the seal is often asserted, but hardly ever justified from an ethical or theological point of view. When a justification is given the arguments used are those of the medieval theologians, and they can seem unnecessarily abstruse and casuistic to the modern mind. It is all too easy today to see the church's assertions about the seal of confession as simply another example of professional confidentiality being applied in an absolute manner which cannot be justified ethically.

It will be clear from preceding chapters that confidences revealed in confession come under the heading of both natural and professional secrets. This provides substantial protection for such confidences, but it does not justify an absolute confidentiality for that which is shared in the confessional. As we have seen, professional confidentiality has its limits. If the absolute nature of the seal of confession is to be justified then there must be other factors which lend extra weight to the obligation to secrecy in this particular instance. There are two such factors. Firstly, confessional secrecy protects the individual's relationship with God. Secondly, the confessor's silence is a reflection of God's forgiveness for sin in Jesus Christ.

(1) To protect the individual's relationship with God:
In Roman Catholic theology the seal of confession is said to arise indirectly from Christ's institution of the sacrament of penance. Even for those who do not recognize the sacramental status of confession, there is enough material in the New Testament to justify both the confession of sins one to another (James 5.16) and the authority of the church to declare sins forgiven (John 20.23; Matthew 9.8; 16.19; 18.18). As Calvin put it,
'It sometimes happens, that he who hears the general promises of God, which are addressed to the whole church, nevertheless remains in some suspense, and is still disquieted with doubts as to the forgiveness of his sins. But if he discloses secretly to his Pastor his distress, and hears the Pastor applying to him in particular the general doctrine, he will be straightly assured where formerly he was in doubt, and will be liberated from every trepidation, and find repose of conscience.' (cit. Thurian, p.21).

In other words private confession is simply another form of what goes on whenever we confess our sins to God and receive his forgiveness. As Christians we live in the constant tension of knowing our sins forgiven in Christ and yet continuing to sin. The blood of Jesus has purified us from all sin (1 John 1.7), yet no one is without sin, and we have a continual need to confess our sins and receive God's forgiveness and cleansing (1 John 1.8-9). Jesus identifies as the primary command of the law the obligation to love God and live in a right relationship with him (Mt. 22.37). To confess and receive God's forgiveness is a necessary part of maintaining that relationship. It is not an unburdening of the individual's conscience to receive psychological release. Rather it is a dialogue between a human being and God, the objective restoration of a relationship which was marred.

We have seen how confidentiality is justified in general terms because it protects the autonomy of the individual, and it protects human relationships. In this case confidentiality protects not only ourselves and our relationships with other people. but also our relationship with God. As Jesus makes clear, this is the primary relationship. We are first of all commanded to love God, and then secondly our neighbour. Confession of our sins to another person is one way in which we repair our relationship with God when it is broken. Absolute confidentiality is not strictly necessary if this reconciliation is to take place, but it is unlikely that people would come to confession if they thought their sins would be revealed. Not to have absolute confidentiality in confession is to put an unnecessary barrier in the path of those seeking to restore their relationship with God. The human institution of confession should reflect the welcome of Jesus: 'Come to me all you who are weary and burdened, and I will give you rest. Take my yoke upon you . . . for my yoke is easy and my burden is light.' (Mt. 11.28-30)

(2) A reflection of God's forgiveness:

If confession is a dialogue between a human being and God, what is the role of the confessor, and how does this affect his obligation to silence? Clearly there are different understandings of the role of the priest or pastor in confession which we do not have the space to consider here. Instead we will take as our model Calvin's understanding of the role of the pastor in confession. Although Calvin did not acknowledge confession to be a sacrament as such, Max Thurian argues that his understanding of confession is completely in line with authentic church tradition.

For Calvin ministers are not only witnesses to a confession taking place between the penitent and God. They are also 'as it were [*quasi*] sureties, to certify our consciences of the remission of sins; insomuch as they themselves are said to remit sins and loose souls' (cit. Thurian, p.33). The word Calvin uses for 'surety' is the same word as is used in Hebrews 7.22 where Jesus is said to be a 'surety and Mediator of a better covenant'. Christ himself is the guarantor of the new covenant, but the minister is in some way (*quasi*) also a guarantor of that relationship between man and God. As Thurian puts it,

> 'it is the duty of pastors, when the conscience of the believer is overburdened, to vouch for the promises of God in Jesus Christ; they stand surety for those promises, guarantee them as it were, when they loose souls by the good news of the gospel in absolution.' (Thurian, p.34).

If this understanding of confession is correct, then the confessor identifies himself very strongly not only with the penitent in his desire to confess secret sins to God, but also with the promises of God through Jesus Christ to remember his sin no more, and to purify and cleanse the sinner, blotting out his sin. As a guarantor of the promises of the gospel he ought to reflect those promises in his own behaviour towards the penitent. He too must 'forget' the penitent's sin, believing it to be truly blotted out, and cleansed from the life of the penitent. If God gives the penitent a new start, so must the confessor. His silence is not, as Aquinas says in one place, the exterior sign of the inward spiritual grace that God has covered over the sins of the penitent. It is not necessary in any way to the forgiveness which God offers the penitent. It is simply that as a minister of the gospel the confessor must act as if he believes that gospel to be true, and that God's forgiveness is effective in the life of the penitent.

Possible limits to the Seal of Confession

If the seal of confessional is justified on the grounds that it is both necessary to protect the individual's relationship with God and as a reflection of God's forgiveness, it is presumably no longer valid when it ceases to perform either of these functions. What this means in practice is that the seal will not apply where the person concerned comes with absolutely no intention of seeking reconciliation and forgiveness.

But this immediately raises a problem. How is the confessor to determine the state of mind of the penitent? Are there any situations in which it is clear that the person is not seeking reconciliation and forgiveness from God? In most cases the confessor will not be able to make a judgement of this kind, and must assume that the confession is genuine. Sometimes, however, there may be reason to question the penitent's motives. The medieval theologians identified two situations where this might be the case. Does the seal apply if the person does not intend to amend his or her life? Does it apply if the person says he or she intends to commit a crime in the future?

Some theologians argue that a firm resolution to commit a sin in the future invalidates the sacramental nature of confession and so frees the confessor from his obligation to silence. Others would say with Aquinas that if the person came seeking forgiveness then the sacrament is valid and the seal of confession still applies, even if there is no desire to change. The latter view stresses the unconditional nature of God's forgiveness. The former view stresses the importance of repentance on the part of the sinner. Both are Biblical emphases which need to be held in tension. We cannot have one without the other. God's forgiveness is given freely and is received by faith, and that faith should manifest itself in a change of heart. Throughout the Bible true repentance implies a changed life, a turning away from sin. If the desire for this is not present at confession then it is doubtful whether the person concerned is really concerned to mend his or her relationship with God. They are not seeking that which the seal of confession is intended to protect.

Imagine the case of a minor member of a mafia-style gang who goes to his priest and confesses a future murder which is to be carried out by the gang. He says he is sorry for the part he will play in that murder, but will not back out now for fear of being hunted down by the gang and killed himself. Here the penitent is seeking forgiveness whilst declaring his firm intention to carry out the sin he is confessing. It is hard to see how this is a genuine confession. He is more concerned to salve his own conscience than to restore his relationship with God. In the process he makes the confessor an indirect accomplice to murder. The confessor must of course seek to persuade him to abandon his intention of committing murder, but in the end he is not bound by the seal, since there is no true desire for a restored relationship with God. The person concerned does not come to confession in an attitude of true repentance.

The same is likely to be the case where the penitent confesses a future crime that is likely to cause severe harm to society in general. In this situation many theologians recommend a general warning, without revealing the name of the penitent. James I used this argument to justify the execution in 1605 of Father Garnet SJ, who knew about the Gunpowder Plot through confession, but failed to denounce it. A modern parallel might be that of an IRA man who confesses to a priest a future bombing campaign. In all these cases it is not the risk to society which justifies the priest revealing the danger. Rather it is the fact that, as in the case of the gangster, the person concerned is not coming to confession in an attitude of true repentance. He does not come with the intention of restoring his relationship with God, and so the seal is no longer protecting that which it is supposed to protect.

It is important to understand that this situation is very different from one in which the penitent comes seeking forgiveness, but knows that even so he may sin again. Take the example of the man who confesses to child abuse. As far as the confessor can tell he is genuinely sorry for what he has done, and is seeking God's forgiveness. He does not want to sin again, though he recognizes his own weakness. In this case the seal of confession does apply, since the man concerned is genuinely seeking to restore his relationship with God. To be afraid of sinning again is very different from a firm intention to sin in the future. Even the risk to the children does not free the confessor from his obligation to silence in this case. He must take the penitent's confession at face value and reflect God's forgiveness in his own attitude towards the person concerned. But he must also take seriously the possible risk to innocent third parties, and insist that the person receives some form of counselling or spiritual direction in order to help him not to sin again. The seal of confession is not an excuse for either penitent or confessor to ignore the social dimensions of sin.

Evidently there are many cases where the confessor will not be able to make a judgement about the state of mind of the penitent, and in these situations the presumption must be in favour of the seal. Only if the penitent actually says that he or she still intends to commit the crime for which forgiveness is sought can the confessor be sure that this person has come to confession with an intention other than that of restoring his or her relationship with God. Confession and absolution are not intended to provide an opportunity to unburden oneself or to obtain some kind of psychological release. Rather they enable individuals to appropriate for themselves the forgiveness of God in Jesus Christ, and so live in a right relationship with God. It is this alone that the seal of confession is intended to protect, and it is only where confession and absolution are regarded in this way that the absolute nature of the seal of confession is justified.